RADIUM GIRL

Wisconsin Poetry Series

Sean Bishop and Jesse Lee Kercheval, series editors

Ronald Wallace, founding series editor

RADIUM GIRL

CELESTE LIPKES

The University of Wisconsin Press

Publication of this book has been made possible, in part, through support
from the Brittingham Trust.

The University of Wisconsin Press
728 State Street, Suite 443
Madison, Wisconsin 53706
uwpress.wisc.edu

Gray's Inn House, 127 Clerkenwell Road
London EC1R 5DB, United Kingdom
eurospanbookstore.com

Printed in the United States of America
This book may be available in a digital edition.

Library of Congress Cataloging-in-Publication Data

Names: Lipkes, Celeste, author.
Title: Radium girl / Celeste Lipkes.
Other titles: Wisconsin poetry series.
Description: Madison, Wisconsin : The University of Wisconsin Press, [2023]
  | Series: Wisconsin poetry series
Identifiers: LCCN 2022028869 | ISBN 9780299341749 (paperback)
Subjects: LCGFT: Poetry.
Classification: LCC PS3612.I6356 R33 2023 | DDC 811/.6—dc23/eng/20220822
LC record available at https://lccn.loc.gov/2022028869

in memory of my father

It is correct to love even at the wrong time.
On rounds, the newborns eyed me, each one
like Orpheus in his dark hallway, saying:
I knew I would find you, I knew I would lose you.
—Spencer Reece, "ICU"

Contents

RADIUM GIRL

Rabbit

Some hats are more likely to contain rabbits.
I flipped bowlers, put my ear to a turban's origami,
fingered the linings of Sunday bonnets,
and came up empty. *I regret to inform you,*
said the silence, *that not all things are possible.*

A cage for every bunny, a hook for every hat,
a pillow for every head that dreams of finding
something hidden. So often we miss it—
once I saw a man holding a Russian doll,
unaware of all the women in his palm.
Even God, bringing light into the world,
was pleasantly surprised to find inside
the white a split

                  of yellow red blue green

sonnet

for my ex-lover with prosopagnosia

you carry a slice of silver   push breadcrumbs
off tablecloths the color of hour-old snow
scattered like rafts across the heated patio
lean toward an old man   a regular   who mumbles
calamari or *gnocchi*   it's hard to tell
twice a night I walk by on my way to the pharmacy
to buy   floss   aspirin   anything small and practical
I can palm in my pocket as you continue not finding me

your memory tethered to identifying tricks
my red bag   my laugh *a porch full of wind chimes*
the way I walk like I'm falling   my face is a stitch
disappearing into a quilt   a word that rhymes
with all other words   unheard   unseen
every night you scrape the tables clean

Rabbit

When the doctor says, "We found something,"
I don't say: "no shit" or "oh thank God,
I've been looking for that sweater everywhere,"
or "*I* have been discovering things for months:
an ember in my stomach, rubies of blood clots
studding the toilet bowl, the meaning
of the word *collapse*." Instead, I nod
and the silence unfolds itself like a paper crane
until the doctor clears his throat and says, "I'm sorry."

/

She is a momentary miracle—
the magician's white gloved fist

around her neck, the hundred open
mouths of velvet-seated gentlemen.

How far away from carrot spears,
tangled hay, honeysuckle petals!

The men's wide eyes are twinned
to the translucent skin inside her ears,

her whiskers, the way her body
lolls into the spotlight's glow.

The magician hoists her, white
and trembling, higher and higher.

Look, his eyes seem to say. *Look
at what I've made from nothing.*

mel·lif·er·ous

   adj. forming or bearing honey

I waited so long
for lunch, spent hours
slipping my fingers
through the chain link
to pick honeysuckle
blossoms, the drops
of nectar like gold coins
in the flowers' ears.

  •

      it was summer

I was wearing a blue dress

      when a bee sees a bloom

it needs to return to

that's how he looked at me

  •

Of all the self-tessellating regular polygons,
a hexagon has the smallest perimeter
of any given area and can distribute loads
without shearing or collapsing.

  •

we toppled into the grass
near the clock tower
& even the moon
honeyed

•

what's it like? I asked
imagine staring at something
terrifying and beautiful he said
now take away the object

•

Sitting in the frame
of the window,
I told him
my nickname:
Bee. Until
I was hospitalized
I never heard my mother
call me Celeste.

•

indefinite period of tenderness—

a phrase lifted
        from *honeymoon*
                or
                        the time between
        a bee landing on a flower
and when it ascends

Rabbit

In the schema I have established
the doctor is the magician
and I am the rabbit.

But I regret to inform you
that there are other possibilities.

God is also the magician
pulling the disease
from the hat of my body.

I am the magician, even,
some nights alone,
finding inside the darkness
a small, trembling thing
I won't acknowledge as my own.
This is someone else's rabbit,
I say, and the silence nods back.

Moon Face

The doctor clicks his pen, says *It's just a phase.*
My fat moon face comes second to the X-rays

he pulls from a folder labeled with my room number.
I'm taking 75 mg of Prednisone a day. It's summer,

and I'm paler than I've ever been. *Lookin' good,*
the doctor says, by which he means: *You could*

look worse. Here in Room 208, I've come to love
men who tell the truth, touch me without gloves,

and let me skimp on barium. My X-ray tech this afternoon
wasn't one. He looked at me as if peering through

a telescope as I, the cold and distant satellite,
moved quietly into his crosshairs. *Hold tight!*

he said. I waited for him to let me breathe again.
Released and back at home, I drift into the kitchen.

I'm white and wide, but never full. I try to sleep.
I think: *My life is compromise* and count sacrificial sheep.

One night I cup a dozen pills inside my palms,
close my eyes, and consider swallowing them all.

Instead, I eat two sandwiches. Out on the night's thin skin,
the white bruise grows, shrinks, blooms again.

Rabbit

As a magician, I promise never to reveal the secret of any illusion to a non-magician, unless that one swears to uphold the Magician's Oath in turn. I promise never to perform any illusion for any non-magician without first practicing the effect until I can perform it well enough to maintain the illusion of magic.

This is the oath.

/

Method 1:

Acquire a top hat and a table with a secret rabbit-sized opening. Line a box with shredded newspaper. Place a bunny in the box attached to the bottom of the table. Cover the table with a tablecloth. Practice with the rabbit until she waits calmly to be lifted into the light, until she knows that *abracadabra* means *here comes the hand*.

Method 2:

Crush charcoal to dust and coat the rabbit until she is the exact degree of dark as the inside of a hat. Deprive her of food and drink for three to four hours to avoid a mess, place her in the hat, and put the hat on your head before you walk on stage. It is not recommended that you wear the rabbit for an extended period of time.

Before the trick is performed, the rabbit must be trained to shut her eyes on cue (snapping one's fingers is the most popular signal). When you tilt the hat so the audience can verify its emptiness—its distinctive lack of rabbit—use the cue so the wet shine of the rabbit's pupils doesn't give her away. Brush off the charcoal discreetly—here, *abracadabra* means *be clean*—and pull her up by the white scruff of her neck.

/

Method 1:

Discovery via interrogation. When did it start. Have you been abroad in the past six months. Do you own or have you recently come into contact with any exotic animals—an iguana, for example. Have you changed your diet since the symptoms began. Is there a family history of stomach problems. Where does it hurt. Have you recently gone swimming in any freshwater lakes or streams. How much does it hurt quantitatively, on a scale from 1 to 10, 1 being normal and 10 being the worst pain you've ever experienced. The questions are asked, but the body is silent.

Method 2:

Collect the dispensable: vials of blood, a cup of warm urine, excrement in a screw-topped canister. Examine the mouth, palpate the abdomen, insert your latexed finger where no finger has gone before. Prior to being presented to the white-coated, there must be a purification. Allow no food or drink for days, save for jugs of polyethylene glycol mixed with Gatorade. Verify the gut's emptiness—a distinctive pink-ribbed cleanness. Collect tissue, take pictures, leave no trace of entry. Everything the body says will be used against you.

Anatomy Lab

I.

You may find it emotionally difficult
to dissect signifiers of personhood,
says the anatomy professor,
meaning these knuckles, these nails
still with dirt underneath them,
this stiff hand I hold as I trim
away skin to the muscles beneath,
thin ropes that, puppetlike, pull
up each finger—their names
abductor pollicis brevis
opponens digiti minimi
a prayer I practice reciting,
my cadaver's palm frozen open,
as if he is asking for something.

II.

You can't just reach in
like an Aztec, says
the anatomy professor,
gesturing where to cut
the cadaver. I break into
the chest, pick the lock
of the ribs, unclip
the clavicle's necklace, lift
the lid of the sternum.
Light illuminates the muscles
between ribs—stained glass
sinew into which the music
of the organ rose, *lub-dub*
lub-dub. I clip the pericardium,

pulmonary trunk & veins,
aorta, vena cavas, until
the gush of formaldehyde
subsides & I can touch
the primal valentine.

III.

Guess he didn't make any films,
says the anatomy professor,
our cadaver poorly endowed
& ravaged by cancer.
We're instructed to *fillet*
the tight skin of his penis,
peel it back like a glove
to reveal the sponge
of its center, deep dorsal vein,
dorsal nerves, & urethra.
The shaft that someone
once hungered to touch,
to fill themselves with,
now sallow & bloodless
& halved by a scalpel.
But it's the hair that strikes me:
a soft mat of curls
dark & thick as my lover's
that I could never
let someone else hold.

Eve Miscarries

The jar of snake legs smashed the night I bled.
I sorted clay from cartilage from bone.
There are words that cannot be unsaid:

let there be light and *of my flesh* and *wed.*
I'm only here so you won't be alone.
The jar of snake legs smashed the night I bled

and thorns stippled the sky above our bed.
The farthest fields beget the seeds you've sown.
There are words that cannot stay unsaid,

so flooded with courage I bowed my head,
confessed, *I can't give you children.* Thrown,
the jar of snake legs smashed. The night I bled

you whispered, *give me back my rib, instead.*
A thousand bent-knee prayers will not atone
for words you should have left unsaid.

Catastrophe behind us and ahead:
the star-pierced sky, the garden overgrown,
the jar of snake legs smashed. The night I bled
I wished that every word could be unsaid.

Rabbit

forcing back the chalk of barium
　　　　pacing the third-floor hallway
of St. Anthony's Hospital
　　　　there is nothing left inside of me
to puke so I retch into the trash
　　　　at one end of the hall then walk
to the other end to heave again
　　　　I memorize the paintings on the wall
an abstract owl followed by
　　　　a still life with grapes then a red house
what art I'd hang if this hall were mine
　　　　I think before my body buckles below
an out-of-perspective mountain

　　　　and my mother comes running

I am falling into a very large hat

　　　　everything black and 10 10 10

/

The Temptation of St. Anthony / Salvador Dalí

caravan of demons
with spindly stilt legs
teeth wide as tombstones
unearthed with a roar

this is one desert of many

I recall only
electric hooves on my chest
my eyes emptying themselves
dear elephants   help
how can you bear to remember

Dove

There is a bird that will sing
both halves of a duet
when its mate dies, but that bird
is not a dove.
   There is a bird
from the swamp of my childhood,
all dinosaur and plume, but that bird
is not a dove.
   There is a bird
that crosses oceans with clouds
of its compatriots, but that bird
is not a dove.
   Negate all of birddom
in search of the most silent, the most docile,
the most willing to forget its form
in favor of a handkerchief, a lit match—

animalia chordata vertebrata aves
     columbiformes columbidae

say this prayer until the white one appears

ne·pen·thes

1. n. drugs mentioned by Homer that allow one to forget sorrow; antidepressants

2. n. a genus of carnivorous plants

monkey cup   lizard drowner
spider eater   poison pitcher
nectared tempter   lidded killer
send the birds back to their maker
wing   shell   bone   tail
feather   webbing   spinner   stinger
little remnants of loss
no one remembers

•

I gathered shells
while he surfed

sand sucking my heels
I watched his body disappear
the wave like a blue eye closing

•

an abbreviated list of things that cannot be unseen:

sparrows crowding the sill
blood on the patio
a glass tipping

my breasts
the apricot moon
his hands trembling

•

Half full at the approach of night,
Lamarck writes, the plant is an urn
into which a bug flies, slipping
from air into syrup,
$\qquad\qquad$ whole days
when he can't get out of bed.
Thickness pins his limbs,
props his eyes open. What I wish
for him always: short night
into morning.
$\qquad\qquad$ I stand at the lip
looking in, until the insect stops struggling.

•

the rim of the seawall
almost complete
the tide at Long Beach
tempered by concrete

no more waves
to drown or surf in
there are side effects
he says   *to everything*

•

wine-dark sea
was the phrase
we were trying
to recall
the evening
we snuck
into the museum
and stood before
the glass case
of rare butterflies
almost touching

•

The first encounter was a miracle.
Past ills were forgotten
as the men watched the pitcher's
opening lid—an eye unafraid—
let everything in.

Dove

columbidae columbiformes
aves vertebrata chordata animalia

> disappears

/

I have a chronic autoimmune illness
named after the man who discovered it
(imagine if God named everything *God*),
Burrill Bernard Crohn. Crohn's disease
is characterized by inflammation
of the gastrointestinal tract.
I am in the hospital because doctors say
I am *failing to thrive*. I weigh ninety-eight pounds
and use the bathroom seventeen times a day.
My father does not say much, but looks at me
with wide eyes when he thinks I am asleep.
My mother takes notes in a yellow legal pad
and twists her wedding ring around and around.
No one asks what makes me happy now
that I can't dance or go to high school or eat fettuccine alfredo.
I watch *Whose Line Is It Anyway?*
and take the hottest shower I can stand
with my face pressed against the frosted window.

I don't remember asking my mother
if I'd ever feel better, but she says I did,
says she went home and pulled the car
into the garage, turned off the car, closed the garage door,
and cried. When I go to sleep, I feel myself slipping
like sand between the twin fists

of an hourglass. Only the yellow legal pad knows
how many times my medications have been switched.
promethazine budesonide mesalamine
azathioprine prednisone sulfasalazine
hyoscyamine dicyclomine ondansetron
—the names of Martian children.

When the doctors believe I am wasting away
by small enough increments, I am released
from the cage of the hospital.
The days shuffle into place like cards
in a deck. I go to class when I can,
take my pills in the bathroom, try to ignore
the girls whispering to each other
about how I have an eating disorder.
A mother of a girl in my dance class
approaches my ballet teacher, says she is *Concerned*
for my well-being. She spends our class
in the lobby gossiping about the latest diet trends.
Fat bitch, my mother says and we smile
and go shopping for jeans that will fit.
Did you know they make size 00? Two zeroes,
for the extra empty. When a boy in my chemistry class asks
if I'm dying, I say *yes*, and everyone leaves me alone.
When teachers pull me aside and ask
if I need extensions on any assignments, I say *no*.
When I ask God if I will feel normal ever again,
I take the silence to mean *maybe*.

Instructions for My Lover

It is advisable to look from the tide pool to the stars
and then back to the tide pool again.
—John Steinbeck

Allow algae to skin the swimming pool
so the water doesn't have to mirror the stars.

When I can't get out of bed, let prayers arc
like pennies flicked into a pool.

Covet cogs and keys, the possibility of machinery.
Prize the compass's thin arms. Disregard the stars.

Emulate the nurse who moves her hands
like silk sinking into a koi-dappled pool.

When the moon is an unpaired parenthesis, do not
touch me. Admire the spaces between stars.

Decide which is more terrifying: a memorial
for the dead or my face in the reflecting pool.

After I'm gone, rediscover the toys of my childhood.
Tangle the jump ropes. Scatter the jacks like stars.

Look to the sea, who hoards things from this life—
starfish reinventing themselves in her tide pools.

Remember the celestial sphere is full
of dead things we still consider stars.

La Brea Tar Pits

The first step's squelch
wasn't enough warning,
nor the muddy pearls
of gas bubbles rising,

nor the slowly sinking bodies,
farther out—a vulture
thrashing viscous wings,
prehistoric horses braying.

On the pit's soft shore,
flattening the weeds to a carpet
with his pacing, a saber-toothed cat
eyed all the beasts prostrate

before him and waded in
with assumed invincibility.
The hunter and the hunted
would not lie so peacefully

until nights upon the ark.
Corpses sunk and soaked
to the bone with tar, cougar
next to elk, falcon below toad—

these deaths being the oldest
chain of misunderstanding:
thirst before hunger, placing
one foot in front of the other.

Dove

my fever is so high I hallucinate
mice circling the IV pole
my dead grandmother dragging
a fork through my Jell-O cup

what do people do I ask the nurse
when they can't stop seeing things
she hands me a stack of paper
and teaches me to fold a crane

/

The type of trickery that women love:
when a caged bird vanishes beneath a cloth
and *one-two-three* reappears unharmed—
a dove cupped in the magician's palm
the way I saw a mother hold her baby's flopped-
back head. *My son, my only son.*

The secret is there are two birds.
The cage, collapsible, yields
to the magician's fist. Pop of bone,
wreck of wings and mangled beak.
The magician pulls another not-dead dove
from deep within his sleeve.

The kind of trickery I need to see: kill
a bird and don't pretend to bring it back.

cousin

i.
under a sheet
in the sunroom
we found it

metal ribbed
black barrel
of a trunk

flaking rust
in your hands
as it opened

its body full
of bolts of cloth
white & stiff

ii.
before the ship left
termini imerese
and her second son
died and she sewed
without a pattern
four baptismal gowns
our great grandmother
packed a steamer trunk
with enough fabric
to make a sail

iii.

easter sunday we set the table

      snapped the cloth in the air

pinned its four corners

      as it buoyed upward

later when you said *leukemia*

      the word was a whiteness

that arced the air between us

      fell   covered everything

iv.

no stranger to the way water
resists the bow of a boat

hesitates the oars
of eight strong men

you cut the river
every morning

the coxswain shouted
a pattern of attack

but the water wanted
to stay whole

v.
no one is allowed
to see you until
as the doctor says

he has been completely replaced

vi.
emptying the house
after the death
of our grandfather

you pulled the bolts
of brittle cream
from the trunk

I scrubbed
its three gold locks
with a toothbrush

wiped clean
the metal bands
around its hull

I couldn't lift it
so you did

dust billowing
into light

vii.
the night before
they left for america
she must have cried
over the body

packing it by candlelight
with expensive fabric
the whitest thing she knew

thick milk
replacing the air

Dove

The doctor asks to speak to me alone.
He perches on the edge of the bed,
smooths the sheets with his gloved hand.
There are some things you should no longer do,
he says. He hands me a list: no popcorn,
no blood donation, no alcohol—two stapled pages
of negations. He says, *I know you are young . . .*
I stare at a spot just above his left shoulder.
But I need to tell you that, well, certain forms
of sexual intercourse are not recommended
for people with your condition. I am fourteen.
I like to read, eat strawberries by the pool,
kiss my dog between his golden ears.
This is just as uncomfortable for me
as it is for you, he says, popping the balloon
of silence. I say, *OK.* I say, *Thank you.* I smile.
I fold two new cranes with staple slits for eyes.

/

According to Lance Burton, the hardest part
of performing the dove act is not the act itself,
but making people care about it.

The magician is trying to fool, he says,
and being fooled is not a pleasant experience.
We are asking people to enjoy being deceived.

Often it is a matter of misdirection.
Even writing this, I have put what I meant to tell you
up my sleeve.

A Kite Addresses Benjamin Franklin

The lightning wants you to know
it reaches for whatever it pleases—
light can strike a woman through a keyhole.

When brilliance grabbed me, I glowed.
At the end of my body—a brass key
the lightning wanted badly. I know

what you couldn't have, you stole:
exquisite sparks that buckled your knees,
glances of a woman through a keyhole,

radiances our eyes can never hold
for long. (Even God looks away, releasing
lightning.) What I wanted you to know:

I saw you kick the shimmering snow
and knock your knuckles raw, pleading
to a woman through the keyhole.

Where the light travels, you cannot go
with this bright an appetite inside your belly,
wanting lightning, wanting to know
how to touch a woman through a keyhole.

Dove

Saint Anthony, perfect imitator of Jesus, who received from God the special power of restoring lost things, grant that I may find [mention your petition] which has been lost. Restore me to peace and tranquility of mind, the loss of which has afflicted me even more than my material loss. Amen.

/

Not just birds, but monuments—
Copperfield made Lady Liberty
vanish one night in 1983.
When the giant sheet lifted,
the statue was gone.

The softness of a woman is suited
to being lost in sheets on a dark night.
I have done it myself without
a single hour of magical training.

The trick is bringing her back,
recalling what once was fact:
the curl of her fingers around a book,
the rough skin of her elbow, the way
her eyes caught the flame and held it.

/

Over the Town / Marc Chagall

His body is a needle—
once, the only kind I knew—
silver sewing stick,

tiny eye the color fits through.
She is a piece of thread
not quite entering his pupil.
Flimsy. There is a seamstress
somewhere that could fix
all this, could lick her
into shape. *Wait,* the birds say,
wait. So suspended over
the quilted town they stay,
closing their eyes in turn,
and saying very little.

/

The dove released after the flood
reappears with an olive leaf
tucked in her beak.
What does it mean?
I count three things:

1. He has given
2. He has taken away
3. Somewhere there is land

＊

Hemicorporectomy

(n.): 1. a radical surgery in which the body below the waist is amputated, transecting the lumbar spine.
2. King Solomon's prescription for justice.

/

During medical school orientation,
I begin a trick that takes years to perfect:
transfiguring the cape of my hospital gown
into a white coat, charming the snowflaked smock
to dissolve. I keep ending up with only half of me
doctor. I'm a turncoat with a stethoscope,
reciting the Hypocrite Oath.
A standardized patient tells us about her pain
and we practice empathic responses—
Women like it when you listen,
says a surgeon. *Nod your head,* he says.
Say things like I can only imagine.

A Pair of Impossible Objects

I. A Frictionless Pulley

> *Bricks of 9 kg and 10 kg hang from a frictionless pulley.*
> *The 10 kg brick is 3 m from the floor when the system is*
> *released. Find the time it takes the brick to hit the ground.*

It doesn't squeak,
      little silent circle

holding one great weight
on the left,

      one great weight on the right.
The string passes over the disk

and the molecules are strangers
in a train station. *Hello-goodbye,*

      you say. Such an easy burden
before the body hits

the floor. That's what we call
the brick in physics: a falling body.

Every body is pulled downward,
      the question is how long

will it take, how quickly
will the quiet halo rotate.

II. A Sharpened Stick of Negligible Mass

*At the bottom of a 200 m high cliff and across a 30 m
wide raging river is a stranded explorer. To send him
supplies from the top of the cliff, you impale the supplies
on a sharpened stick of negligible mass and attach it to the
front of a rocket. What minimum speed must the rocket
have before impact in order to save the explorer's life?*

It exists because I will it—
a branch so light it cracks

      with the weight of a sparrow.
      No mass to subtract,

just the multiplying of momentum,
the curve of calculator buttons

      pushing back against the thumb.
      At night my snug-shut eyes

can't stop seeing him
across the river's rush,

      the stick like a phantom limb
      divorced from its trunk.

I got the problem wrong. I guessed
because I knew that's what you'd do.

      I'd make a forest weightless
      if I thought it could save you.

Hemicorporectomy

Scenario 1: The day we bisect the cadaver's face, I am cutting two women in two. The boys flip her onto her back, cursing her weight, four inches of slick yellow fat over her torso. We elevate her head with a wooden block, pull a sheet up to her neck, the claws of her hands dangling over the edge of the table. *Check for dentures,* says the professor. *They're impossible to cut through.* I run my gloved finger over her gums, the dryness startling me back into my body. Everything that should be wet, isn't—her amber skin, her half-closed eyes between which one of the boys draws a line with his finger from scalp to clavicle. *Here,* he says, and lets the saw shriek through her forehead.

Scenario 2: The day we bisect the cadaver's face, I stay in bed.

cam·pa·nol·o·gy

n. the study of bells

My sister was married under the sound—
a church by the sea, white gown barnacled
to her body. She dragged the train behind her
like a mother pulling a petulant child
away from the water.

.

I climbed
the clock tower

before
I held him

beneath it
before

he was
the bell

I wanted
to ring

.

Meditation:
the teacher tells us to track the chimes
until they collapse—each *dong*
a wave swooning into silence.

•

the sort of stillness he loved   a calculus exam

proofs rustling awake

under flakes of eraser

$$p(x) = \frac{1}{\sigma\sqrt{2\pi}}\, e^{-\frac{1}{2}\left(\frac{x-\mu}{\sigma}\right)^2}$$

dark curve we huddled under

•

Curls of prosciutto,
green olives, bread.
After dinner, we fall
asleep holding each other
until the doorbell
startles us apart.

•

For years I misheard
the lyrics from the soundtrack
of *The Diving Bell and the Butterfly*—

I fell into the ocean when you became my wife

I fell into the ocean and you became my wave

•

He is oceans away. I make the bed,
run, breathe, eat my spinach.
A bell must be in tune with itself.
Without him here, it is hard even to listen.

•

no music without anatomy
       ear lip waist tongue
when I touch myself
       the feeling rings
memory lapping endlessly

Hemicorporectomy

Before Illusion Device
patent number 1,458,575,

before Criss Angel pulled apart
a woman on a park bench,

Horace Goldin premiered
his trick at the Hotel McAlpin.

The box was three-people deep—
too large for deception,

said critics. But his mistake
was selecting a bellboy

with a jaunty red drum of a hat
to saw into halves.

Truncating a man, they said,
who wants to see that?

/

We practice on illusions of people:
an actor cradling a baby doll
(*She won't stop crying!* mom says),
a cadaver whose only identifiers are
65—female—pulmonary failure,
a high-tech male mannequin
voiced by a woman (*We're short on staff,*
the facilitator apologizes).

In one session the mannequin
will not stop seizing.
We scatter to apply oxygen,
press our hands
to its heaving plastic chest.
It's our fourth week in school
and we know nothing of medicine.
My own heart matches
the mechanized throb,
panic filling me to the brim:
I don't know what I'm doing
I don't know what I'm doing
my stethoscope trembling
until the director calls *Time!*
and tells us our patient is dead.

Hospital through a Teleidoscope

They die in an instant, in the middle of the night;
the people are shaken and they pass away . . .
—Job 34:20

In bed, I shake the world by turning glass.
Twisting the plastic tube, I shut one eye,
watch the people break apart and pass

out of my lens. This is my morning mass—
mosaic of pills, white nurses floating by.
In bed, I shake the world. By turning glass,

I split the mother's dying son, the brass-
necked stethoscope, the doctor's tucked-in tie.
I watch the people break apart and pass

my curtained room. I fill six test tubes, wineglass-
thin, with blood. I fast. I sleep. I lie
in bed. I shake. The world, by turning glass

to dust, scatters what we thought would last.
The mother down the hall keeps screaming, *Why?*
I watch the people break apart and pass

away. That night, the doctor cups my mass,
benign, like bread between his hands. I cry
in bed. I shake the world. By turning glass,
I watch the people break apart and pass.

Hemicorporectomy

The first woman to be sawn in half has received less publicity than the magician who first presented the illusion.

/

The Temptation of St. Anthony / Paul Cezanne

his eyes shielded

                     from the trap

of her curves

       she lifts the sheet

                  revealing a secret:

her skin is a beacon

          nothing can pierce it

/

How do they do it?
is less interesting than *Why?*

But I'll humor you, reader:
in one version, the box rests

on a hollowed-out table
that the assistant sinks into,

the blade barely grazing her crotch.
In another, the box is open-ended.

The sequined assistant contorts
into the box's upper half after pushing

a mannequin's legs out the back.
The box is cut by a saw and pulled

apart: the top half of her real,
the bottom half fake.

This is the split, the body as diptych.
This is the most vulnerable part of the trick.

Snail

She plucks the one
with the slowest glide,
the endless scrolled home,
and cooks the flesh
until the sky goes slack.
The man is unimpressed.
The meal, a mouthful
at most, cultivates
an emptiness.
                Their bodies take
to one another, knife
to apple skin. The nick.
Then the slow spiral,
red and unbroken.

Hemicorporectomy

My first patient is despondent not to be dead.
She unfurled her femoral artery into the bathtub—
a practiced trick. She is a mortician, used a blade from her kit.
I knew what to do, she says. *I knew where to cut.*
The gash in her groin gapes between stitches,
and I stand looking in as if on the edge of a cliff.

/

I swear to fulfill, to the best of my ability and judgment, this covenant:
I will apply, for the benefit of the sick, all measures which are required, avoiding
those twin traps of overtreatment and therapeutic nihilism.

I will remember that there is art to medicine as well as science, and that warmth,
sympathy, and understanding may outweigh the surgeon's knife or the chemist's
drug.

I will not be ashamed to say "I know not," nor will I fail to call in my colleagues
when the skills of another are needed for a patient's recovery.

/

But one slice
was never enough.

The audience's appetite
was kaleidoscopic,

fragment-hungry,
wanted her

piecemeal.
Thus, Radium Girl:

the woman is
pinned in a box,

perforated with swords
& cut neatly in four

like a pill too strong
to take whole.

Escape

*(v.): c. 1300, "free oneself from confinement, extricate oneself from trouble" . . .
from Vulgar Latin *excappare, literally "get out of one's cape, leave a pursuer
with just one's cape"*

/

Instructions for Exiting the Psychiatric Ward:

1. Display your ID above hip level, as to be seen easily from the nursing
station.
2. Scan the area around the exit for other providers and patients. When the
elderly Korean woman kneels by the door picking invisible strings off the
floor, her FLIGHT RISK RESTRICT TO UNIT bracelet twisting around and
around, gently direct her to the common room. When the man bangs his
fist on the door's small window and shouts I'M GOING TO CARPET BOMB YOU
SHITHOLES, wait for security.
3. Signal politely to the unit secretary that you would like to leave.
4. Approach the door.
5. Wait for a dull buzz. Look around to make sure you aren't being followed.
6. Open the door and walk through it briskly. Push the handle firmly behind
you.
7. Approach the second door.
8. Wait in the vestibule for the electronic hum.
9. Ensuring that no one attempts to enter the vestibule from the main hospital,
open the second door and exit.

/

PLEASE PARDON ANY INCIVILITY IN THIS LETTER. IT HAS BEEN RUSHED TO YOU UNDER STRESS OF BUSINESS AND **WRITTEN IN THE DRESSING ROOM**. THEREFORE ALL FORMALITIES, LIKE, DEAR SIR, DEAR MADAME, ETC., HAVE BEEN OMITTED—NOT TO BE CURT OR BRUSQUE; BUT THAT IT IS DEEMED BETTER TO LET YOU HEAR FROM ME IN A LETTERGRAM OF A FEW WORDS THAN NOT AT ALL.

CORDIALLY YOURS,

HOUDINI

ROSABELLE—answer—tell—pray, answer—look—tell—answer, answer—tell

infusion room praise song

when the IV bag shrinks moonlike over my head
and purple blossoms in my elbow crook
people stare at me the way I'd look
at a three-legged dog in the bad part of town

when my dog dies I will not have a heart big enough to bury her
I commission you to do it
scrape of the shovel hitting clay
dirt arcing into the air the way they say the soul does after death

during infusions I use my shoulder to hold the phone to my ear
when you call the nurse is tying the tourniquet
the nurse is tying the tourniquet I say
and because you know I hate this part
for the same reason I hate long enclosed slides at water parks
all that tight darkness
you say *let me tell you a story*

your grandfather went to war with a bad heart
his doctor said *you won't come back anyway*
he pinched kentucky soil into a matchbox
kept it in his shirt pocket as he cut through clouds
watched bombs fall behind him like silver fish
through the waterfall of the air
when he was shot down by germans
the soldiers stripped him
shook out his shirt and found the matchbox
what is this they asked
what is this in german sounds like branches snapping under boots
what is this what is this what is this
a whole tree ground to mulch

they beat him against the wall
in war it is easy to mistake a matchbox full of dirt
for a matchbox full of explosive powder

when I was very sick
hope was a dog lost in the night
I stood in the doorway
I let the doorway prop me up
I could not call the dog back
this is what happens when
we don't teach each other our names

CELESTE LIPKES
on a band around my wrist
remember this
while I am well
I am hoarding everything for later
pool of pink petals we fall in together
dumplings dripping soy sauce into my lap
reflection of my newly baptized face in the lake

this is the dirt my pockets are full of

who can blame us for wanting to die
on our own land

Escape

In the classification of escape performance,
the most respected genre is *Escape or Die*.
The flirting with conclusion never ends:
death by drowning, death by falling,
death by suffocation. The goal is escalation.
But even Houdini learned his limits the night
he couldn't break the handcuffs' secret.
The London *Daily Mirror* challenged him
to escape from cuffs that took a locksmith
five years to create. Trapped, Houdini kissed
his wife on stage, the silver key slipping
between their lips.
                              Nights on call in the ICU,
I walk laps past bodies ensnared in tubes,
bags of blood like vultures suspended overhead.
Every evening I count the dwindling brass coins
of my patient's platelets while his wife ices
cups of ginger ale he will never drink.
When his face becomes a mask of itself,
she lies down in bed and sings him a hymn.
This is the greatest magic trick: escaping
the body gracefully. Never underestimate
the training required to know when to signal
for the key.

/

Code:

1: pray	*6: please*
2: answer	*7: speak*
3: say	*8: quietly*
4: now	*9: look*
5: tell	*10: be quick*

al·bes·cent

adj. becoming or passing into white

there was
a moment
when I saw
the glass
tipping
and thought
I can stop this

then milk
everywhere

•

White noise is the hardest to block,
as it contains a wide range of frequencies
all possessing the same intensity.

•

how to forget

      that beautiful blanching

the whitest part of him

      pouring into my hands

•

Faces shift like clouds. I'm at the ocean
again with my doctor: him: my sister.
The water scrambles over our feet,
frothing to nothing.

•

When asked
about his pain,
the patient
with a brain injury
says he is walking
down the street
and a man
follows him,
dragging a roller
filled with white paint,
painting over
everywhere
he's been,
blanking out
windows,
the sidewalks,
erasing even
his name.

•

my gifts to him, in reverse order:

noise canceling headphones
bowl of coconut ice cream
handful of Q-tips
mad-lib on a faded receipt
(some emptiness for you to fill)

•

when my face
            goes pale
blood
is rushing   elsewhere

Escape

It is hard to let go of what you have made.
You can do it, the nurse says over and over.
Nine months of confidential creation,
now this long labor.

/

The Eye, Like a Strange Balloon, Moves Toward Infinity / Odilon Redon

Sick kids' eyes
ascend like this.
And who can blame
the pupils,
those twin Houdinis,
for slipping from the body's
tendon trap to test
the firmament,
where water vapor
still can choose:
rain or sleet or snow?
Lashes to the stratus,
sockets swelling in the wind
up, up they go.
We're losing him,
the doctor shouts,
as our faces, heavy
as bags of sand,
bear down upon the bed.

/

Dorothy Dietrich, commonly called the Female Houdini, grew up in rural Pennsylvania with six brothers. Before she became the first woman to catch a bullet in her mouth, before she slid out of straightjackets and cut men in half, she ran away from her abusive father at the age of thirteen. This was her first escape act.

Two Small Fish

I see you once
a month,

the calendar
a net I sink

my hands into.
I know how to let

two small fish
feed five thousand,

how to kneel
at the stained glass

of a gill: our forks
tangling, my lips

at your throat.
Alone, I multiply

snatches
of brightness

until a night
catches us

not yet frightless,
& the last thing

I see is your eyes'
golden lattice,

blue breaking
behind it.

Escape

Rosabelle, sweet Rosabelle,
I love you more than I can tell.
Over me you cast a spell.
I love you, my sweet Rosabelle.
—inscription in Bess Houdini's wedding ring

/

When I ask the meaning of the baby's name
she says, *Night sky*. When I ask the name
of the man in the room, she says,
Cousin. When she is ready to push,
she sweats darkly through the cloud
of her hijab, does not hold the nurse's hand.

It is lonely to enter the world this way,
strangers in gloves grappling with your neck,
the darkness like a favorite vase shattered.
With a gush you escape,
screaming on the breast of your mother.
The cord roots you still to her insides,
its pulse a soft rain retreating.
The nurse hands me the scissors.

/

In the schema I have established
the patient is the magician
and illness is the handcuffs.

But again: there are other possibilities.

I am also the illusionist
leaving behind the cape
of my hospital gown.

Even poems are a trap
to break free from.
In this way you are also a magician.
If you find a way out,
please let me know.

Alphekka

broken crown of stars

I grew up in the perforated dark,
bright-struck, cheek pressed against sleek telescopes.
I swept across the Milky Way's faint arc
& knocked my flashlight beam past Pisces' ropes,

Aquarius, the Hunter's lucent hips.
I tripped a lot back then—my head tipped back,
my opened mouth an annular eclipse.
I stood in awe of things that broke through black.

At school, I nightdreamed through the classroom's hum,
connected dots behind closed eyes until
they filled my skull's domed planetarium.
The sticker stars on homework didn't thrill

me anymore, so I put them on my tongue.
They clung like notes, a golden song unsung.

They hung like golden notes, a song unsung
until I swallowed & shat an astral melody,
told no one. One night my mother strung

a popcorn chain around the aspen tree,
remembering last winter when she'd found
a sparrow stiffened into slack-beaked sprawl.

Behind the red-roofed barn, I heard the sound
of dirt flung back & saw mom's shadow crawl
across the snow as she lay down to rest

the shoebox casket in the ground. She hummed
"Ave Maria," crossed herself, & pressed
a stone into the snow-slush mound. I thumbed

my frostbit nose at flakes falling from the sky.
The steady heavens winked her thousand eyes.

Steady heavens: blink. Your thousand eyes
are fixed on all this earthbound misery:
a duck's snapped neck, the estuary dry,
my body flimsy as an effigy.
Which is to say: you watched me almost die,
dear universe, how I once observed a bee—
belly-up & wild—writhe inside
a mason jar of broken combs and honey.

This is the sweetest sort of drowning, this
is all I thought the night the feeding tube
went down: viscous wings, the nectar's glue,
the scoop, salvation in a slotted spoon.
Evenings when my lids clench shut like fists,
thank God's lost eye, the socket of the moon.

Escape

When Dorothy performs
the trick Houdini refused
to attempt, she is dressed
in all white and moves
as if underwater.
She climbs the stage
and a man points a rifle
into her mouth.
When the shot is fired,
she swims backward,
settling to the ground
like an anchor
around which the sand
of the crowd rearranges.

/

ROSABELLE: believe

/

When I was very ill, I spent evenings locked
in the bathroom. I had Prednisone-induced insomnia
and my eyelids were tangled window blinds
I couldn't close. Those nights when wellness felt impossible
I sat on the yellow tile next to the toilet
and watched videos of card tricks:

A woman from the audience signs the Queen of Spades
with a black marker and shuffles it into the deck,
only to have the magician pull the card from his wallet.
Then he rips the Queen in fours
and presses the confetti into the woman's hand.

You know what happens next.
Not the part where the Queen reappears untorn
in the middle of the deck, but the part
where I am finally given infusions of medication
and can visit the bathroom rather than taking up inhabitance,
drink strawberry milkshakes instead of barium chalk
that makes my insides glow.

Not when the magician shows the woman the card
and points to her signature, but the part
where I call my mother to tell her
I have been accepted into medical school
and her shouts kaleidoscope down the hallway.

Not when the magician says, *Is this your card?*
(Because she has signed it, it is hers.)
But the part where my patient waiting to be discharged
asks, *Is today the day?*

And when she says, *Yes, it is*—
not the clapping, but the amazement before it.

Acknowledgments

Thanks to the following journals for first publishing these poems, some of which appear in a different form: *Bellevue Literary Review, Blackbird, Iron Horse Literary Review, The Labletter, Lunch Ticket, Measure, Rattle, SAND,* and *Unsplendid.*

Thanks to the Johns Hopkins University, the University of Virginia, Bucknell University's Stadler Center, the Atlantic Center for the Arts, and the Yale Department of Psychiatry for their support of this project. Gratitude to the dozens of teachers who shaped this manuscript, particularly Marcia Childress, Rita Dove, Kathy Graber, Mary Jo Salter, and Lisa Russ Spaar.

Much love to many friends with keen eyes and ears who read these poems in their early incarnations. Thanks especially to Jake Ricafrente, who started it all, and Sebastian Doherty and Chelsey Weber-Smith, whose talents are only outweighed by their kindness. I would never have survived medical school without Drs. Jason Barnes, Phil Chapman, Jenika Ferretti-Gallon, Will Hall, Bobby Reitz, Phil Sasser, and Yael Tarshish.

Thank you to my parents for never making me choose between science and poetry summer camp.

Gratitude to my doctors and my patients; it is an honor to care and be cared for.

To feel known by someone else is a kind of magic. The thickest thesaurus does not have enough synonyms for *thank you* for Christian Detisch.

Notes

"sonnet" is based on an anecdote from a *Radiolab* episode titled "Falling."

The end quotation in "ne·pen·thes" is by Carl Linnaeus, translated by Harry Veitch.

"cousin" is in memory of Todd.

The physics problems in "A Pair of Impossible Objects" were adapted from *Fundamentals of Physics* by David Halliday.

"infusion room praise song" is for Amanda and Dr. Mary Harris.

Graphing the function in "cam·pa·nol·o·gy" results in a bell curve.

The coded telegram in "Escape" was adapted from a document from Harry Houdini's archives held at the Harry Ransom Center. "Rosabelle" was a term of endearment for Houdini's wife, Bess, based on a love song Bess sang during the Houdinis' first show together. Before Harry Houdini passed away, he and Bess created the code "ROSABELLE: Believe" as a way for Harry to communicate with Bess after his death. Bess held yearly séances on Halloween after her husband died, in hopes of hearing this phrase. Before her death, Bess asked a friend to carry on this yearly tribute; this tradition was eventually passed to Dorothy Dietrich.

Wisconsin Poetry Series

Sean Bishop and Jesse Lee Kercheval, series editors

Ronald Wallace, founding series editor

How the End First Showed (B) • D. M. Aderibigbe

New Jersey (B) • Betsy Andrews

Salt (B) • Renée Ashley

Horizon Note (B) • Robin Behn

About Crows (FP) • Craig Blais

Mrs. Dumpty (FP) • Chana Bloch

Shopping, or The End of Time (FP) • Emily Bludworth de Barrios

The Declarable Future (4L) • Jennifer Boyden

The Mouths of Grazing Things (B) • Jennifer Boyden

Help Is on the Way (4L) • John Brehm

No Day at the Beach • John Brehm

Sea of Faith (B) • John Brehm

Reunion (FP) • Fleda Brown

Brief Landing on the Earth's Surface (B) • Juanita Brunk

Ejo: Poems, Rwanda, 1991–1994 (FP) • Derick Burleson

Grace Engine • Joshua Burton

Jagged with Love (B) • Susanna Childress

Almost Nothing to Be Scared Of (4L) • David Clewell

The Low End of Higher Things • David Clewell

Now We're Getting Somewhere (FP) • David Clewell

Taken Somehow by Surprise (4L) • David Clewell

Thunderhead • Emily Rose Cole

Borrowed Dress (FP) • Cathy Colman

Dear Terror, Dear Splendor • Melissa Crowe

Places/Everyone (B) • Jim Daniels

(B) = Winner of the Brittingham Prize in Poetry

(FP) = Winner of the Felix Pollak Prize in Poetry

(4L) = Winner of the Four Lakes Prize in Poetry

Show and Tell • Jim Daniels

Darkroom (B) • Jazzy Danziger

And Her Soul Out of Nothing (B) • Olena Kalytiak Davis

My Favorite Tyrants (B) • Joanne Diaz

Midwhistle • Dante Di Stefano

Talking to Strangers (B) • Patricia Dobler

Alien Miss • Carlina Duan

The Golden Coin (4L) • Alan Feldman

Immortality (4L) • Alan Feldman

A Sail to Great Island (FP) • Alan Feldman

The Word We Used for It (B) • Max Garland

A Field Guide to the Heavens (B) • Frank X. Gaspar

The Royal Baker's Daughter (FP) • Barbara Goldberg

Fractures (FP) • Carlos Andrés Gómez

Gloss • Rebecca Hazelton

Funny (FP) • Jennifer Michael Hecht

Queen in Blue • Ambalila Hemsell

The Legend of Light (FP) • Bob Hicok

Sweet Ruin (B) • Tony Hoagland

Partially Excited States (FP) • Charles Hood

Ripe (FP) • Roy Jacobstein

Last Seen (FP) • Jacqueline Jones LaMon

Perigee (B) • Diane Kerr

American Parables (B) • Daniel Khalastchi

Saving the Young Men of Vienna (B) • David Kirby

Conditions of the Wounded • Anna Leigh Knowles

Ganbatte (FP) • Sarah Kortemeier

Falling Brick Kills Local Man (FP) • Mark Kraushaar

The Lightning That Strikes the Neighbors' House (FP) • Nick Lantz

You, Beast (B) • Nick Lantz

The Explosive Expert's Wife • Shara Lessley

The Unbeliever (B) • Lisa Lewis

Radium Girl • Celeste Lipkes